STEP BY STEP TO CALVARY

PRAYING THROUGH THE STATIONS OF THE CROSS

D0837749

STEP BY STEP TO CALVARY

PRAYING THROUGH THE STATIONS OF THE CROSS

ANGELA M. BURRIN

the WORD among us®

The Word Among Us
9639 Doctor Perry Road
Ijamsville, Maryland 21754
www.wordamongus.org
ISBN: 978-1-59325-049-2

Cover and book design: David Crosson
Art taken from *The Way of the Cross*, by Giandomenico Tiepolo (1727-1804)
Photo credit: Cameraphoto/Art Resource, N.Y.

Made and printed in the United States of America

Library of Congress Control Number: 2004113907

Nihil obstat: The Reverend Michael Morgan
Censor Librorum
August 26, 2004

Imprimatur: +Most Reverend Victor Galeone
Bishop of Saint Augustine
August 26, 2004

CONTENTS

INTRODUCTION

ONE OF THE MOST POPULAR and treasured traditions of the Catholic Church is the Stations or Way of the Cross. Since the early days of Christianity, devout pilgrims have walked and prayed along the Via Dolorosa in Jerusalem, the road that Jesus walked as he carried his cross to Golgotha. This was only natural: the followers of Jesus desired to be in the same physical places as their Savior as he carried his cross to his death.

As the vast majority of Christians could never travel to Jerusalem, the stations were a way to recreate that experience wherever they lived. Over time, probably by the sixteenth or seventeenth century, the fourteen stations developed as we know them today and as we find them in Catholic churches and chapels all over the world.

Today, this devotion is offered by most parishes during Lent and Holy Week, the liturgical times of the year when we most want to recall the passion and death of Christ. But since Jesus' death and resurrection are the central mysteries of our faith, we can pray the stations any time of the year. However we choose to pray the Way of the Cross—whether alone or with others, using formal or spontaneous prayers—this devotion allows us to contemplate for an extended period of time the suffering and passion of our Lord.

Over the years, many beautiful prayers have been written for the Way of the Cross. While focusing on the same event, each offers a slightly different perspective on how to view Jesus and his suffering and death.

Like other versions of the Stations, the meditative passages in *Step by Step to Calvary* are intended to help readers grasp the reality of Jesus' suffering along the Via Dolorosa. In this book, each of the fourteen stations also tries to help readers come to know Jesus more deeply. This is done in two ways: using a title that describes who Jesus is, such as Emmanuel or the Good Shepherd; and highlighting one of his attributes, such as gentleness, humility, or obedience.

After visualizing Jesus' passion and coming face to face with the Lord, these stations provide an opportunity for repentance and healing in a specific area. Each station ends with intercessory prayer. Jesus' resurrected life is celebrated in a litany of praise at the conclusion of the fourteenth station. Don't feel obligated to pray through all the stations at one sitting, as the Lord may have something specific to say to you at one particular station.

The many relevant biblical references provided in each station may inspire you to look up these passages on your own. In praying through these stations, Scripture can come alive for you. Every Scripture verse can affirm the reality that God loves you unconditionally and that through the death and resurrection of his Son Jesus, you can enter into a deeper personal relationship with him.

As you pray the stations in *Step by Step to Calvary*, may the Lord bless you abundantly.

Angela M. Burrin
The Word Among Us Press

RECALLING AND RELIVING THE PASSION THROUGH THE STATIONS OF THE CROSS

BY FR. JUDE WINKLER, O.F.M. CONV.

A t a conference several years ago, I was responsible for a display of children's books. All throughout the afternoon, parents approached and bought books for their children. Occasionally a parent would tell a child to choose any book on the table—but only one. The smallest children inevitably chose the same book: The Stations of the Cross. I had thought that the image of the crucified Jesus on the cover would frighten them, but in their innocent simplicity, they could see beyond the horror of the cross to the love it expresses.

It is that love we celebrate when we pray the Stations of the Cross. We are not just commemorating events that occurred two thousand years ago. We are entering into the passion of Christ to experience how he poured out his life and love for the forgiveness of our sins.

The Origins of the Stations

The stations seem to have originated in the pious practice of pilgrims to the Holy Land who visited the sites of the life, suffering, death, and resurrection of Jesus. Among other sites, pilgrims would visit Golgotha and the tomb, both of which were soon enclosed in the Church of the Holy Sepulchre. These pilgrims found that there was something powerful in actually touching the place where Jesus died and rose.

We have an account, in fact, of a Spanish nun named Egeria who visited the Holy Land in the fourth century A.D. She describes the liturgy that was celebrated at the holy sites. On Sunday, for example, the celebrant would read the biblical story of the

9

resurrection of the Lord. She wrote, "When the reading is begun, there is so great a moaning and groaning among all, with so many tears, that the hardest of heart might be moved to tears for that the Lord had borne such things for us." Likewise, she describes how on Good Friday, "the emotion shown and the mourning by all the people at every lesson and prayer are wonderful; for there is none, either great or small, who, on that day during those three hours, does not lament more than can be conceived, that the Lord had suffered those things for us."

This practice of commemorating Jesus' passion was so esteemed that churches and monasteries in Europe began to establish reproductions of the holy sites. Thus, those who could not afford the long and arduous pilgrimage to the Holy Land could nevertheless experience a spiritual visit there.

Two events further fostered this devotion. The first was the Crusades. Many people traveled to the Holy Land, and many more heard of their travels and longed to experience what they had described, if only in a symbolic manner.

The second stimulus occurred in 1342, when the shrines throughout the Holy Land were entrusted into the care of the Franciscan Friars. They prepared proper accommodations and obtained special indulgences for the pilgrims so that their visit would be as spiritual as possible. They also spread devotion to the passion of Jesus throughout the Christian world.

The Franciscans and Their Influence

Franciscans have always had a great love for anything associated with the life and death of Jesus. St. Francis helped popularize the Christmas crib when he set up a living manger scene in Greccio, Italy, in 1223. He also loved to meditate upon the passion of Jesus, even writing his own Office of the Passion to commemorate it. Francis saw in the birth and death of Jesus the two key moments when Jesus' humanity and humility were most clearly visible. He saw in them the summit of Jesus' surrender to God, a surrender of total love.

St. Francis was so moved by this love that it became visible. When he was at Greccio, he was so inflamed with gratitude that those around him saw him holding the child Jesus in his arms, even though there was no child present at the scene. Likewise, when he was on Mt. Alvernia several months later, Francis received the stigmata, the very wounds of Jesus in his flesh, thus making his body a living remembrance of the passion. The lover, St. Francis, came to resemble the beloved.

From their very beginning, then, the Franciscans have seen it as their duty to foster devotion to the stations and the Christmas crib. At first, the stations that they built were located outside churches, but by the middle of the seventeenth century, they were being placed indoors instead. Franciscans were so identified with this devotion, in fact, that until recently they were the only ones who were given the privilege of blessing newly erected stations.

How to Pray the Stations

There are many different ways to pray the stations. Many parishes celebrate them as a community, especially during Lent. While suffering tends to separate and isolate us, commemorating Jesus' suffering as a community tends to bind us together. It makes us more fully one with him and with each other.

There are, of course, times when we pray the stations by ourselves, more as a silent meditation. Praying them in this way can be a deeply intimate experience, giving us the sense that we are walking alongside Jesus on his way to the cross.

The walking associated with the stations is also a form of prayer in itself. In a sense, we are praying with our feet. All too often we pray only with our minds. But walking the stations helps make our prayer more complete as we bring our bodies in line with our minds, similar to the way Jesus did on his way to Golgotha and the way Francis learned to do when he received the stigmata.

Remembering and Reliving

It's important to know that when we pray the stations, we are not only recalling ancient history. The Jewish people believe that by recounting a past event, we can somehow participate in that event. This is called *anamnesis*, and it is the basis for our understanding of the Mass. At the Eucharist, we are present in our own churches, but we are also somehow present at the Last Supper, before the cross, and at the empty tomb. We pass beyond our present time and mystically experience a bit of eternity.

This is also what we do when we pray the stations. We are not only telling the story, we are also entering into it. Jesus' love for us as expressed in the stations and our love for him bridge the gap between what happened then and our lives today. We see Jesus fall under the weight of the cross and are horrified at his pain. We become Veronica and offer to wipe his face. We stand with Mary as she watches her beloved son die. No longer disinterested bystanders, we, like Francis, become united with Christ.

Our Passion

Jesus told his disciples to take up their crosses and follow him, and the stations give us the opportunity to do just that. We die to ourselves when we reflect upon our sin and remember that Jesus died for our forgiveness. As we remember the sufferings of Jesus, we can also recall how we have sinned against God and each other.

When we remember how Jesus was judged, we can ask whether we have misjudged others. As we commemorate the three falls of Jesus, we can recall the times we have fallen into sin as well as the times we have seen others fall and did not help them.

We also take up our cross in the stations by joining our sufferings to those of Jesus. Suffering often makes us feel as if we were upon a cross with no one to help us. But in the stations we are reminded who is on the other side of that cross: Jesus, who is always with us.

The stations can also encourage us to take up the cross of the challenge to live our faith in a more profound manner. They help us find the courage to reject those things that separate us from God's love, to be crucified to the world so that we can give ourselves to God and others more fully.

Finally, the stations offer us the opportunity to be in solidarity with the suffering of the world. When we pray the stations, we can exercise compassion—a word that means "to suffer with." We can take other people's suffering upon ourselves so that they no longer have to carry their burdens alone.

Never the Same

There are certain events in our lives that change us forever. The death of a loved one, a wondrous triumph, a new insight— all of these can leave an indelible mark on us. The stations are just such an event. How could life be the same after we have experienced so much love? How could we look at ourselves or the world around us with the same eyes after having gazed upon the One who was pierced for our sins? Jesus literally loves us to death. As we contemplate what Jesus did for us through his passion, we are filled with overflowing gratitude, a willingness to live in that love, and to share that love with all we meet.

THE FOURTEEN STATIONS

Art taken from *The Way of the Cross,*
by Giandomenico Tiepolo (1727-1804)

The First Station:
Jesus Is Condemned to Death

The Second Station:
Jesus Accepts His Cross

The Fifth Station:
Simon of Cyrene Helps Jesus
to Carry His Cross

The Sixth Station:
Veronica Wipes Jesus' Face

The Ninth Station:
Jesus Falls a Third
Time

The Tenth Station:
Jesus Is Stripped of
His Garments

The Eleventh Station:
Jesus Is Nailed to the
Cross

The Third Station:
Jesus Falls the First Time

The Fourth Station:
Jesus Meets His Mother

The Seventh Station:
Jesus Falls a Second Time

The Eighth Station:
Jesus Speaks to the
Women of Jerusalem

The Twelfth Station:
Jesus Dies on the
Cross

The Thirteenth
Station: Jesus Is
Taken Down from
the Cross

The Fourteenth
Station: Jesus Is Laid
in the Tomb

I adore you, O Christ,
and I praise you, because by your
holy cross you have redeemed
the world.

This is my Son, the Beloved, with whom I am well pleased." Jesus received these words of affirmation from his Father as he was being baptized in the Jordan River by John the Baptist (Matthew 3:13-17; Mark 1:9-11; Luke 3:21-22). His hidden life was now over, and his public ministry had begun. He chose disciples, taught the crowds about the kingdom of God, healed the sick, raised the dead, and performed other miracles. After years of waiting, the Scriptures were being fulfilled—the Messiah had come! But not everyone accepted Jesus. The religious leaders were challenged by his teachings and accused him of blasphemy. The political activists quickly discovered that he would not join them or promote their cause. Judas, one of Jesus' disciples, agreed to betray him for the price of thirty pieces of silver.

Finally Jesus is arrested in the Garden of Gethsemane. First he is taken to the high priest and then before a council of chief priests and teachers (Matthew 26:47–27:2). Now we see Jesus standing before Pilate, the Roman governor of occupied Israel. There is pressure on Pilate to condemn Jesus to death. He hesitates. Pilate considers Jesus innocent and undeserving of death. He decides to exercise his right to release a prisoner. After all, it is the Feast of Passover, when it is the custom for the governor to grant freedom to a prisoner chosen by the people. When he asks the crowd whom to release, they shout "Barabbas!"—a known murderer. Pilate is disturbed, but he doesn't want to risk a riot so he publicly washes his hands of the matter. He orders Jesus to be whipped and then hands him over to the people (Matthew 27:11-26; Mark 15:1-15; Luke 23:1-25; John 18:28–19:16).

Jesus, Who Are You?

You are Emmanuel, "God with Us" (Isaiah 7:14; Matthew 1:23). Jesus, you who are the second Person of the Trinity took on our nature and was born of the Virgin Mary to fulfill your Father's plan of salvation. You still live among us, and you promise to be with us always: "Where two or three are gathered in my name, there am I in the midst of them" (Matthew 18:20). "I am with you always, to the close of the age" (Matthew 28:20). Jesus, you are with me here, right now. I bind myself to you. I place my hope and trust in you.

Jesus, Show Me Your Face

You are humble. You were born in a stable, known as the son of a carpenter, and baptized in the river Jordan as a sinner. You were an unpaid preacher, homeless, and then falsely accused. Standing before Pilate, you spoke only to confirm that your kingdom is not of this world (Matthew 27:11). "Yet he opened not his mouth; like a lamb that is led to the slaughter" (Isaiah 53:7). Jesus, you are God, and yet you allowed yourself to be condemned and sentenced to death by those whom you created in your own image to know and love you (Genesis 1:26-27). "Being found in human form he humbled himself and became obedient unto death, even death on a cross" (Philippians 2:8). Jesus, you humbled yourself for me.

Jesus, I Repent

I come before you now to ask for your forgiveness and healing love. Jesus, forgive me for the times when I've "washed my hands"—ignoring the truth—and have chosen to act for personal gain. I am sorry for the times I've jumped to conclusions and accused someone who was innocent. Father, I ask forgiveness for criticizing others. If I have ever been falsely accused or treated unjustly, Holy Spirit, heal me of those painful memories.

Jesus, I Pray

I turn to you in prayer and intercession. Jesus, *Emmanuel*, thank you that you did not come to judge us but to save us (John 12:47). Clothe me with your humility.

At this **First Station** I pray for all those who hold positions of authority—the pope, leaders of churches and nations, parents, educators, police officers, and business employers. Holy Spirit, give them your wisdom.

I love you, Jesus, whom I love above
all things. I repent with my whole heart for
having offended you. Never permit me
to separate myself from you again.
Grant that I may love you always,
and then do with me as you will.

(Stations of the Cross by St. Alphonsus Liguori)

I adore you, O Christ,
and I praise you, because by your
holy cross you have redeemed
the world.

Pilate has ordered Jesus to be whipped. Jesus is taken into the courtyard of the Praetorium, stripped of his garments, and tied to a pillar. The soldiers take turns striking Jesus—a total of forty times—with strips of leather tied to pieces of broken bone. Jesus' shoulders, back, arms, and legs are covered with gaping wounds. What excruciating pain he experiences! Yet the guards are not satisfied; they want to be entertained. They drape a purple robe over Jesus' shoulders, push a crown of large, twisted thorns into his head, and place a reed in his right hand. "Hail, King of the Jews!" they mockingly chant (Matthew 27:27-30). Blood trickles down from the crown of thorns, matting Jesus' hair and beard and staining his face. Perhaps Jesus remembers his prayer just hours before in the Garden of Gethsemane, when he told his Father: "If it be possible, let this cup pass from me; nevertheless, not as I will, but as you will" (26:39).

The soldiers now drag a large wooden cross into
the courtyard. They place it in front of Jesus.
He willingly and silently accepts it (John 19:17).
The moment Jesus had predicted has come to
pass (Luke 9:22; John 12:27-33). He knows that
by his death on these two beams of wood, he will
redeem the world and offer to *all* the free gift
of eternal life. He is to be the atoning sacrifice
for our sins (1 John 4:9-10). What an incredible
plan our heavenly Father had for our salvation!
"God so loved the world that he gave his only
Son, that whoever believes in him should not
perish but have eternal life" (John 3:16).

Jesus, Who Are You?

You are the Son of God. You called your Father "Abba." You taught us that we too are sons and daughters of God and can approach him by praying "Our Father" (Matthew 6:9-13; Romans 8:14-15). You spent nights in intimate prayer with your Father, seeking direction and strength for your ministry (Mark 1:35). What love the Father had for you! I am grateful that my heavenly Father's love for me is so passionate that he allowed you, his only Son, to carry a cross through the streets of Jerusalem to the hill of Calvary.

Jesus, Show Me Your Face

You are patient. Jesus, you accepted your cross with patient endurance. You, the Son of God, suffered the abuses of the Pharisees and Roman guards, standing silently as the soldiers mocked you and beat you. You were patient with all those you encountered in your public ministry: with the crowds who kept following you (John 6:5-12); with your disciples who were discussing who was the greatest (Mark 9:33-37); and even with the Pharisees and Sadducees, who sadly didn't understand your mission (Matthew 22:23-46). Jesus, even when I offend you repeatedly by my sin, you patiently welcome me back to you.

Jesus, I Repent

I come before you now to ask for your forgiveness and healing love. Jesus, for the times when I've been impatient, angry, or have complained about my life, forgive me. Holy Spirit, heal me of wanting things done my way and in my time. Father, I ask for the patience to accept your will and timing for my life. I want to use my present circumstances to draw nearer to your Son, Jesus, and to grow in holiness.

Jesus, I Pray

I turn to you in prayer and intercession. Jesus, *Son of God*, thank you for accepting the cross for my salvation. I now accept your invitation to take up my cross and follow you (Matthew 16:24-26).

At this *Second Station* I pray for all those people who are carrying a personal cross of suffering: a serious illness, the death of a loved one, the breakdown of a marriage or a family relationship, the loss of a job, or the stress of living with a spouse or child addicted to drugs or alcohol. Holy Spirit, heal them of fear and anxiety. Comfort and strengthen them.

Lord Jesus Christ, Son of God,
have mercy on me, a sinner.
(The Jesus Prayer)

I adore you, O Christ,
and I praise you, because by your
holy cross you have redeemed
the world.

Jesus is bent under the weight of the cross as he leaves the courtyard of the Praetorium. He begins dragging it along the narrow, uneven stones that pave the streets of Jerusalem. It is one-third of a mile to Calvary, the hill of execution outside the city walls. The mid-morning air is hot and sultry. Crucifixions are a common occurrence, but they still draw the crowds. Today three men will be executed.

The rough beams of wood cut into Jesus' flesh. Pain shoots through his head as the cross bangs against his crown of thorns. "Surely he has borne our griefs and carried our sorrows" (Isaiah 53:4). Suddenly, Jesus staggers and falls. Some in the jostling crowd gasp in horror. Others laugh at his weakness. For a few minutes, Jesus lies motionless on the ground. The only help he gets is from the soldiers, who roughly pull him

to his feet by the rope around his waist. Abuse
spills out of their mouths.

Jesus is completely undeserving of this treatment. He is not a criminal; he is innocent. Even
Judas, his betrayer, recognized this fact: "I have
sinned in betraying innocent blood" (Matthew
27:4). Why is this happening to Jesus? Why is
the innocent Son of God condemned to death?
"He was wounded for our transgressions, he
was bruised for our iniquities; upon him was
the chastisement that made us whole, and with
his stripes we are healed" (Isaiah 53:5). Adam's
disobedience and fall from grace led to our
separation from our heavenly Father. Now Jesus
falls from the weight of the cross, the weight of
our sin. Through his death, he will reconcile us
to his Father (Colossians 1:21-22).

Jesus, Who Are You?

You are a Friend of Sinners. It was you who proclaimed that you came to call not the righteous but sinners to repentance (Luke 5:32). Even though you were criticized for associating with sinners, you ate with them (Matthew 11:19), healed them (Mark 2:5), and called Matthew—a dishonest tax collector—to be one of your twelve disciples (Matthew 9:9-13). Jesus, as I watch you fall, I know that I am a sinner, too. I was in your thoughts as you walked toward the hill of Calvary. You knew how I would live my life. You knew the decisions I would make that would hurt myself and others. And still you loved me.

Jesus, Show Me Your Face

You are innocent. Jesus, you bore the sins of humanity but committed no sin yourself (Hebrews 7:26). During your public ministry, even the evil spirits proclaimed your innocence (Mark 1:23-27). Although innocent, you did not defend yourself before Pilate (15:5). Jesus, as you hung between two guilty thieves, there was no anger, bitterness, or resentment in your heart. When you died, the centurion at the foot of your cross said, "Certainly this man was innocent!" (Luke 23:47). Jesus, because of your innocence, you could be the spotless Lamb who was sacrificed for my sins.

Jesus, I Repent

I come before you now to ask for your forgiveness and healing love. Jesus, like the soldiers, I have not always controlled what comes out of my mouth. Father, I am sorry for the times I have failed to reverence your name or used crude or abusive language. Forgive me when I've gossiped about someone. Holy Spirit, help me to guard my tongue, especially when I am provoked by others. Heal me of any unresolved anger.

Jesus, I Pray

I turn to you in prayer and intercession. Jesus, *Friend of Sinners*, I rejoice that you have accepted me as your friend. Give me the courage to reach out to others as you have reached out to me.

At this *Third Station* I pray for anyone who is addicted to drugs, alcohol, gambling, or pornography. Holy Spirit, give them the courage to admit their addiction and seek treatment. Protect those who have been set free from their addictions from being tempted again. Sustain with your strength those who run recovery programs.

Eternal Father, for the sake of Jesus' sorrowful passion, have mercy on us and on the whole world.
(The Chaplet of Mercy)

I adore you, O Christ,
and I praise you, because by your
holy cross you have redeemed
the world.

Shaken and bruised from the fall, Jesus summons the strength to get up, lift up his cross, and continue walking. A woman emerges from the crowd to greet him. Startled onlookers recognize her as Mary, Jesus' mother. Mary wants to be close to her son to comfort him with her presence. She wants to assure Jesus that she can endure the sword that is piercing her heart (Luke 2:35). Although brokenhearted, the Father's grace is sufficient for her to accept the incredible hatred and cruelty being heaped on Jesus. Perhaps Mary whispered to Jesus, "My Son, this is the day we spoke about as we studied the words of the prophets. You are doing your Father's will." The very presence of his mother causes Jesus to lift his head. As he looks into her sorrowful eyes, his heart is torn. How he wishes she did not have to undergo the pain of seeing him in this wretched state. But her *fiat*—her yes to God—meant that she would experience the suffering of the cross as well as times of joy (Luke 1:26-38). Mary's loving face encourages Jesus. Did he whisper from his parched mouth, "Mother, I love you," before being ordered by the soldiers to keep moving?

Jesus, Who Are You?

You are the Son of Mary. Jesus, throughout your life, Mary pondered the things that she witnessed and treasured them in her heart (Luke 2:19, 51). She recognized that despite her "low estate," all generations would call her blessed (1:46-55). Jesus, at your time of greatest need, you experienced the tender and courageous presence of your mother. You invite me to know Mary as my mother so that I, too, can be comforted by her presence in my life—especially when fear, discouragement, despair, and loneliness are about to overwhelm me.

Jesus, Show Me Your Face

You are gentle. Jesus, you are so approachable. You told the crowds, "Come to me, all who labor and are heavy laden, and I will give you rest . . . for I am gentle and humble in heart" (Matthew 11:28-29). Children had a special place in your heart, and you asked for them to be brought to you for a blessing (19:13-15). At Jacob's well in Samaria, you spoke gently to the woman who was living with a man who was not her husband (John 4:4-42). You did not condemn the woman caught in adultery (8:3-11). Gentle Jesus, today I come to share with you all that is on my heart and mind. (Take some time to do this.)

Jesus, I Repent

I come before you now to ask for your forgiveness and healing love. As you walked toward Calvary, your mother was there to comfort you. Forgive me, Jesus, for those times when I've abandoned others when they most needed my presence. Help me to be sensitive to the needs of others, especially when they are hungry for my love and encouragement. Forgive me, Father, for the times when I've been harsh to someone when I should have been gentle instead. Holy Spirit, I pray for the gift of gentleness toward all those in my family and to all those whom I will meet today.

Jesus, I Pray

I turn to you in prayer and intercession. Jesus, **Son of Mary**, thank you for giving your mother to the Church. Mary, I ask you to be my mother, and I consecrate myself to you.

Jesus, at this *Fourth Station* I pray for all mothers, especially single mothers, those with sick children, and those who lack material or emotional support. Heavenly Father, just as you entrusted your precious children to these mothers, increase their trust in you and in your loving provision for them. Holy Spirit, help all mothers to know the Father's love in a personal way. Forgive and heal those mothers who have had abortions. Whether living or deceased, I lift up my own mother to you. Keep her in your loving care.

Holy Mary, Mother of God, pray for us sinners, now and at the hour of our death. Amen.

(The Hail Mary)

I adore you, O Christ,
and I praise you, because by your
holy cross you have redeemed
the world.

The Fifth Station

SIMON OF CYRENE HELPS JESUS
TO CARRY HIS CROSS

Jesus wearily drags the cross through the gate leading out of the city of Jerusalem. After Mary's brief encounter with Jesus, she is comforted by some of the women who cared for him during his public ministry. Together they stay as close to Jesus as the guards will allow. The soldiers are fearful that Jesus' strength will give out before he can be crucified. Each step looks as if it will be his last. Where are his friends? Has he been completely deserted (Matthew 26:56)? Why doesn't anyone come forward to help him? A commotion breaks out. The crowds watch as the soldiers seize a farmer visiting the city, who is known as Simon of Cyrene. They force him to help Jesus carry the cross (Mark 15:21).

STEP BY STEP TO CALVARY

Simon has been chosen by God the Father to help Jesus, his beloved Son. What a divine appointment! When Simon awoke that day, surely he didn't know who and how he would be called upon to help. Did Simon know of Jesus and his ministry? What went through his mind when the soldiers cornered him? Was he angry? Did he fear what people would think if he helped a man on his way to his execution? Or was his heart open and filled with compassion? Was he grateful that he had the physical strength to help Jesus? Were any words exchanged between Jesus and Simon? All unanswered questions. But we know that the Father in his tremendous compassion made provision for Jesus so that he would no longer have to carry the weight of the cross alone. ❦

Jesus, Who Are You?

You are the Word of God. Weak, bleeding, and limping toward your death, you needed the aid of a bystander, Jesus, to help you carry the cross. Yet you are the revealed Word of your Father. "God . . . has spoken to us by a Son" (Hebrews 1:1-2). Unlike Simon, we cannot meet you on the road to Calvary, but we can meet you through Scripture. As you walked the earth, you spoke words given you by your heavenly Father (John 14:10). Your words and actions make known to us God's saving and merciful love. Holy Spirit, touch my heart and mind with the Scriptures as I slowly reflect on them in prayer and hear them at Mass.

Jesus, Show Me Your Face

You are compassionate. As your Father was compassionate in bringing you the help of Simon of Cyrene, so you are compassionate with us. Day after day in your public ministry, you spoke healing words to the sick (Matthew 14:14; Mark 1:40-45). You reached out to those who were grieving. You accompanied Jairus, the synagogue ruler, to his home when his daughter was dying (Mark 5:22-23, 35-43), and you brought back to life the son of a widow (Luke 7:11-17). Jesus, your compassion melts my heart and makes me want to be like you.

Jesus, I Repent

I come before you now to ask for your forgiveness and healing love. Jesus, Simon's help came at just the right time for you. Often when I see people in need, I ignore them. My excuses are that I'm too busy, that I don't want to get involved, or that someone else will help them. Forgive me, Father, for my laziness and hardness of heart. Holy Spirit, heal me of self-centeredness and fear of getting involved. Give me an opportunity today to serve someone with an act of kindness, a word of affirmation, or the promise of prayer.

Jesus, I Pray

I turn to you in prayer and intercession. Jesus, *Word of God*, thank you for all the words of compassion you speak to me through the Scriptures, my family, and friends. Fill my heart with the same compassion so that I may be Christ to them.

At this **Fifth Station** I pray for all who serve others, especially caregivers of the elderly and disabled. I pray also for all those serving in the armed services, fire, rescue, and police departments. Holy Spirit, give them patience and wisdom, and protect them from all danger.

> You are God: we praise you;
> You are the Lord: we acclaim you.
> (The *Te Deum*)

I adore you, O Christ,
and I praise you, because by your
holy cross you have redeemed
the world.

Now accompanied by Simon of Cyrene, Jesus continues his agonizing trek to Calvary. The heavy wooden beams, lying against his sore and bleeding shoulders, make it impossible for him to look up. But his eyes are on the goal set before him by his Father: obtaining eternal life for all who will accept him as Lord and Savior (John 17:1-5). When his pace is too slow for the soldiers, they mercilessly kick him or strike him with their leather strips to his already bruised body. His face is sweaty, grimy, and contorted with pain. Blood is still trickling down from the crown of thorns onto his forehead and dripping into his eyes, nearly blinding him. "His appearance was so marred, beyond human semblance, and his form beyond that of the sons of men" (Isaiah 52:14). How much more can Jesus endure?

Suddenly, a woman is by Jesus' side. She has pushed through the crowds. Her quick move startles the soldiers. Their shouts of "Get back!" are unheeded. A hush comes over the bystanders. Some recognize the woman as Veronica and wonder, "What is she doing?" With eyes only for Jesus, Veronica takes off her veil and gently wipes the blood from his forehead, eyes, cheeks, and mouth. For a moment, Jesus is comforted. "As you did it to one of the least of these my brethren, you did it to me" (Matthew 25:40). Did any words pass between Jesus and Veronica, or did her loving touch say it all? Her faithful love is rewarded. Jesus' face is imprinted on Veronica's veil.

Jesus, Who Are You?

You are the Prince of Peace. Just as Veronica's gesture brought you a moment of comfort and peace, you are the bearer of peace to our hearts. You told your disciples, "Peace I leave with you; my peace I give to you; not as the world gives do I give to you" (John 14:27). You ask us to have peace with one another (Mark 9:50; Hebrews 12:14-15). Jesus, when you shed your blood on the cross, peace was restored between God and us (Colossians 1:20). Jesus, I ask for peace in my heart today. You know the circumstances in my life that cause me unrest and anxiety. You know my innermost thoughts, struggles, and fears. Comfort me with your peace.

Jesus, Show Me Your Face

You are faithful. Veronica was faithful to you as she risked the abuse of the Roman soldiers to comfort you. Her faithfulness was a response to your own faithful love, a love that reaches out to all. You never discriminated against anyone. You touched and healed those with leprosy (Matthew 8:1-4; Luke 17:11-19). Israel was under Roman occupation, yet you healed the sick servant of a centurion (Matthew 8:5-13). You even allowed your feet to be washed and kissed by a prostitute (Luke 7:37-50). Jesus, thank you for your faithfulness to me. I know you will never reject me.

Jesus, I Repent

I come before you now to ask for your forgiveness and healing love. Jesus, Veronica looked up at your face. Forgive me for not choosing to seek your face in prayer. Father, I repent for my indifference, and for not making time every day to come into your presence. Holy Spirit, free me of any doubts or temptation to believe that my heavenly Father does not hear me in prayer or does not desire to have an intimate relationship with me. Help me to push through the constant noise and distractions of daily life—and my own thoughts—to choose to seek and dwell on the face of Jesus.

Jesus, I Pray

I turn to you in prayer and intercession. Jesus, *Prince of Peace*, I praise you for filling my heart with peace when I draw near to you in prayer. Help me to carry your peace to an anxious and restless world.

At this **Sixth Station** I pray for all those who instruct others in faith and prayer—priests, religious sisters, catechists, and parents. Holy Spirit, pour out a special blessing today on those who have taught me about the sacraments, Scripture, prayer, and the love of God. (Take a few minutes to give thanks for each person.)

Lord, may this sacrifice, which has made our peace with you, advance the peace and salvation of all the world.

(Eucharistic Prayer III)

I adore you, O Christ,
and I praise you, because by your
holy cross you have redeemed
the world.

J esus continues to lose blood from his many open wounds. Those following him shudder at the trail of blood he leaves behind him. The brutality Jesus has suffered since the previous night has taken a tremendous toll on his strength. The pain in his head from the thorns is excruciating and constant. The muscles in his arms and legs ache and cramp spasmodically. His breathing is labored. Although just cleansed by Veronica's veil, Jesus' face is once again streaked with blood, sweat, and dirt. "He had no form or comeliness that we should look at him, and no beauty that we should desire him. He was despised and rejected by men; a man of sorrows, and acquainted with grief" (Isaiah 53:2-3).

Jesus' steps become more and more unsteady. He staggers under the weight of the cross—even with Simon's help. He falls a second time. His body is pinned under the cross. How can it be that Jesus, for whom all things were created, is lying face down in the dirt? "All things were created through him and for him" (Colossians 1:16). His mother looks on, and again she feels the sharp piercing of a sword through her heart. More kicking and lashes are delivered by the soldiers, and their mouths overflow with crude obscenities. "I gave my back to the smiters, and my cheeks to those who pulled out the beard; I hid not my face from shame and spitting" (Isaiah 50:6). Callously the soldiers yank Jesus to his feet.

Jesus, Who Are You?

You are the Good Shepherd. Jesus, we see you fall again under the weight of the cross and know that you willingly undergo this suffering so that you can claim us as your own. "He himself bore our sins in his body on the tree, that we might die to sin and live to right-eousness. . . . For you were straying like sheep, but have now returned to the Shepherd and Guardian of your souls" (1 Peter 2:24-25). You told the people, "I am the good shepherd; I know my own and my own know me" (John 10:14-15). Just as a shepherd knows the cry of his sheep, so you know my cries—for heal-ing, peace, direction, and joy. Jesus, I long to hear and recognize your voice. Please be the shepherd of my soul.

Jesus, Show Me Your Face

You are omniscient—all knowing. Jesus, on the road to Calvary, as you suffered and struggled, you knew that you were fulfilling the Father's mission to redeem us. You did it out of love for us, your sheep. Jesus, the Good Shepherd, you know your sheep. You know what is in our hearts. You saw that Zacchaeus' heart was softening (Luke 19:2-10), and that the heart of the rich young man was struggling to follow you (Mark 10:17-27). You knew that the bleeding woman who touched the hem of your garment was desperate for healing (5:25-34), and that Peter was sorry for having denied you three times after your arrest (14:66-72). Jesus, you know everything about me—both the good and the bad—and still you love me.

Jesus, I Repent

I come before you now to ask for your forgiveness and healing love. Jesus, there are times when I feel as if the sins in my life are too big for you to forgive. I can't even forgive myself. Jesus, help me to know, deep in my heart, that all the suffering you endured on the way to Golgotha truly redeemed me and that I am truly forgiven. I repent for questioning your merciful love. Holy Spirit, heal me of all doubts by pouring into my heart the transforming love of my Father in heaven. Father, if there is one particular sin I still struggle with and can't imagine you forgiving, give me the courage to talk to a priest.

Jesus, I Pray

I turn to you in prayer and intercession. Jesus, *Good Shepherd,* I'm so grateful that you are the Shepherd and Guardian of my soul. Help me to listen to and follow you all the days of my life.

Jesus, at this *Seventh Station* I pray for all those who suffer from physical or mental illnesses. Loving Father, heal them and provide them with appropriate medical care. Jesus, send your angels to protect those who are severely depressed and who may attempt suicide today. Holy Spirit, direct those who administer the programs and organizations that care for the sick.

O my Jesus, forgive us our sins, save us from the fires of hell, and lead all souls to heaven, especially those in most need of your mercy.

(The Fatima Prayer)

I adore you, O Christ,
and I praise you, because by your
holy cross you have redeemed
the world.

JESUS SPEAKS 8 TO THE WOMEN
OF JERUSALEM

To many of the people of Jerusalem, Jesus is but another condemned criminal. But off to one side, a small group of women huddle together. They are wailing and beating their breasts. How can it be that Jesus, who brought such hope into the lives of so many, is on the way to his death? It doesn't make sense. Only a few days before, he had ridden triumphantly into Jerusalem on a donkey. The excited crowds had lined the streets, waving palm branches and singing, "Blessed is he who comes in the name of the Lord! Hosanna in the highest!" (Matthew 21:1-9). As Jesus approaches the women, he stops. They are shocked at the depths of suffering reflected in his eyes. His dry throat and mouth make it almost impossible for him to speak. But he takes the opportunity in faltering whispers to gently teach the women. "Daughters of Jerusalem, do not weep for me, but weep for yourselves and for your children" (Luke 23:27-28).

When Jesus began his public ministry in Galilee, he proclaimed, "The kingdom of God is at hand; repent, and believe in the gospel" (Mark 1:15). Now, with only a few hours to live, his message is the same. "For behold, the days are coming when they will say, 'Blessed are the barren, and the wombs that never bore' . . . For if they do this when the wood is green, what will happen when it is dry?" (Luke 23:29, 31). Jesus foresees the destruction of Jerusalem. Time is running out for the inhabitants of the city. Even on his way to his death, Jesus invites them to seek forgiveness for the ways they and their children have disobeyed God's commands. Jesus wants everyone to live a life of holiness (John 17:6-26). He longs for all of us to be with him in heaven for all eternity.

Jesus, Who Are You?

You are the Good Teacher (Mark 10:17). Throughout your public ministry, you urged people to repent and believe. You continually sought opportunities in the synagogues, on hillsides, and in people's homes to talk about your Father and his plan for us, his children. You taught as one having authority (Matthew 7:29). Jesus, after washing your disciples' feet at the Last Supper you said, "You call me Teacher and Lord; and you are right, for so I am" (John 13:13). Jesus, I ask you to be my Teacher.

Jesus, Show Me Your Face

You are righteous. Jesus, you are pure, holy, and sinless (1 Peter 3:18). Your teachings and parables show us how we too can make choices to be holy in our everyday lives. Jesus, you encourage us on our spiritual journey by telling us that there is great rejoicing in heaven over one sinner who repents (Luke 15:1-10). Jesus, help me to make decisions that reflect your truth. When I don't, give me a repentant heart and assurance of your forgiveness.

Jesus, I Repent

I come before you now to ask for your forgiveness and healing love. Father, you gave us the Ten Commandments because you loved us (Deuteronomy 5:1-21). Jesus, you gave us a new commandment to love one another (John 13:34). I repent for having disobeyed these commandments. Jesus, give me the grace to courageously examine my conscience. I ask for an opportunity to confess *all* of my sins in the Sacrament of Reconciliation, where you await me with open arms. Holy Spirit, I need the grace of this sacrament to resist Satan's temptations. Heal me of the hopelessness that I can't overcome certain sinful habits.

Jesus, I Pray

I turn to you in prayer and intercession. Jesus, *Teacher*, renew my mind as I read the Scriptures. Help me to embrace all your commandments as gifts you give to help me lead a fruitful, joy-filled, and holy life.

At this *Eighth Station* I remember the youth of the world. Jesus, I pray that they open their hearts and invite you into their lives. I bring to the foot of your cross all those young people who belong to gangs, have run away from home, are addicted to drugs and alcohol, or are caught up in prostitution. Holy Spirit, deliver them from the grasp of Satan. Father, protect and encourage those who are trying to be obedient to their parents and the laws of society.

Thy kingdom come, they will be done,
on earth as it is in heaven.
(The Lord's Prayer)

I adore you, O Christ,
and I praise you, because by your
holy cross you have redeemed
the world.

The Ninth Station

JESUS FALLS A THIRD TIME

The noonday sun is high in the sky. Jesus is dehydrated; it has been hours since he has had anything to drink. He barely has enough energy to put one foot in front of the other. The soldiers, impatient with his progress, tug harder at the rope around his waist in the hope of quickening his pace. This causes him to gasp for breath and lurch from side to side. A few more yards, and his excruciating walk will be over. But even a few steps are too much for Jesus. He has no strength left. "I am poured out like water, and all my bones are out of joint; my heart is like wax, it is melted within my breast" (Psalm 22:14). Jesus falls a third time.

Jesus' mother Mary has seen him fall. He lies motionless under the cross. The pain experienced by Jesus as the soldiers brutally drag him to his feet is matched by Mary's emotional suffering as she witnesses the ill treatment of her son. Mary is comforted by the women who have accompanied her. In stark contrast to Mary's agony is the mounting excitement of the bystanders, some of whom are already watching the two criminals as they are being prepared for crucifixion. It will be but a short time now until Jesus will fulfill his own words: "Unless a grain of wheat falls into the earth and dies, it remains alone; but if it dies, it bears much fruit" (John 12:24).

Jesus, Who Are You?

You are the Bread of Life. Jesus, you are that grain of wheat who has now become our heavenly food—a food that satisfies our every need. You told the crowds, "I am the bread of life; he who comes to me shall not hunger, and he who believes in me shall never thirst" (John 6:35). Jesus, help me always to cling to that truth. At the Feast of the Passover—the last meal you ate with your disciples—you took bread and said, "This is my body which is given for you. Do this in remembrance of me" (Luke 22:19). You gave your body to us on the cross and in the Eucharist. Thank you for this most amazing gift!

Jesus, Show Me Your Face

You are generous. Jesus, your generosity knows no bounds. In your earthly life, you always gave yourself so fully to everyone. You placed the needs of others before your own. You changed the water into wine at the wedding in Cana (John 2:1-11). On one occasion you fed five thousand people and on another four thousand because you didn't want them to go home hungry (Mark 6:35-44; 8:1-9). Your heart was touched when you saw the generosity of a widow (Luke 21:1-4).

Jesus, help me to be generous with my time, talents, and money.

Jesus, I Repent

I come before you now to ask for your forgiveness and healing love. Jesus, forgive me for the times I've been indifferent—both to the suffering you experienced as you carried the cross to your crucifixion and to your true presence in the Eucharist. Increase my faith in the Blessed Sacrament to heal me—spiritually, emotionally, and physically. Holy Spirit, heal me of my lukewarmness. Place in me the fire of your love, and make me eager to receive you in word and sacrament at Mass and to sit before you in adoration. Father, I praise you and give you thanks for all the blessings in my life, especially the blessing of the Eucharist. (Take a few minutes to do this.)

Jesus, I Pray

I turn to you in prayer and intercession. Jesus, *Bread of Life*, I love, adore, and thank you. Help me to appreciate your overwhelming generosity every time I receive you in the Eucharist.

At this *Ninth Station* I pray for those who work in humanitarian causes all over the world—in orphanages, halfway houses, shelters, soup kitchens, and worldwide relief organizations. Holy Spirit, empower them to carry out all the work you have entrusted to them. Father, I pray that they will be channels of your love and grace.

> Christ has died, Christ has risen,
> Christ will come again.

(Memorial Acclamation after the Consecration)

I adore you, O Christ,
and I praise you, because by your
holy cross you have redeemed
the world.

J esus' death march is over; he has reached his destination. Now on Calvary, the Lamb of God will be sacrificed as the atonement for our sins. Dark clouds are beginning to roll across the sky, partially covering the sun. The soldiers remove the cross from Jesus' shoulders. Simon of Cyrene, his task completed, blends into the throng of onlookers. Jesus stands motionless. Sounds of pounding hammers and spine-chilling screams from the two criminals being nailed to their crosses momentarily stun the crowd into silence. A soldier gives Jesus a mug of cheap wine. He tastes it, but when he realizes it is mixed with gall, he refuses to drink it (Matthew 27:34).

Jesus is now subjected to another indignity: He is stripped of his clothing. The soldiers, devoid of any sense of decency or gentleness, roughly rip off the outer garment. A second or third tug is needed where areas of his clothing are stuck to his body with congealed blood. More pain. More humiliation. "Though he was in the form of God, [he] did not count equality with God a thing to be grasped" (Philippians 2:6). Another sword pierces Mary's heart. Naked except for a loincloth, Jesus awaits his execution. But first the soldiers throw dice to decide who will get his tunic. "They parted my garments among them, and for my clothing they cast lots" (John 19:24; Psalm 22:18).

Jesus, Who Are You?

You are the Lamb of God. Jesus, as the soldiers strip away your clothing, you are the Lamb being made ready for slaughter. John the Baptist said you were the Lamb of God who takes away the sins of the world (John 1:29). The Israelites had offered the blood of animals in sacrifice and cleansing (Leviticus 16:15, 17:11; Hebrews 9). Now as the sacrificial Lamb of your Father, you shed your blood for me. "Know that you were ransomed from the futile ways inherited from your fathers . . . with the precious blood of Christ, like that of a lamb without blemish or spot" (1 Peter 1:18-19). Jesus, with your precious blood, you have saved me!

Jesus, Show Me Your Face

You are obedient. Jesus, you could have called down a legion of angels to protect you (Matthew 26:53). However, you choose to be obedient to your Father. "For as by one man's disobedience many were made sinners, so by one man's obedience many will be made righteous" (Romans 5:19). Jesus, as a child you were obedient to Mary and Joseph (Luke 2:51). You offered up prayers and petitions to your Father, and you were heard because of your obedience (Hebrews 5:7-10).

Jesus, you alone could say, "I have kept my Father's commandments and abide in his love" (John 15:10). Father, I want to take my every thought captive and make it obedient to Jesus Christ (2 Corinthians 10:5).

Jesus, I Repent

I come before you now to ask for your forgiveness and healing love. Jesus, forgive me for stripping people of their dignity by my inappropriate thoughts, words, and actions. Cleanse me with your precious blood. Holy Spirit, heal me of all prejudices. Father, help me to think about and treat everyone as your child and my brother and sister in Christ.

Jesus, I Pray

I turn to you in prayer and intercession. Jesus, *Lamb of God*, you were stripped of everything of this world except your inexhaustible love for me. Strip from me anything in my life that keeps me separated from you.

At this **Tenth Station**, I pray for all who have been "stripped" through famine, natural disasters, war, terrorism, or economic failure and find themselves homeless, in refugee camps, shelters, or sleeping on the streets. Holy Spirit, quell their fears, comfort them with your loving presence, and through the generosity of others provide for all of their needs.

Behold, this is the Lamb of God who takes away the sins of the world. Happy are those who are called to his Supper.

(Prayer before Communion)

I adore you, O Christ,
and I praise you, because by your
holy cross you have redeemed
the world.

11

JESUS IS NAILED TO THE CROSS

It is time for Jesus to be nailed to the cross he has carried to Golgotha. The soldiers have laid it on the ground near the two criminals, who are already suspended on their crosses. Just as Jesus is about to collapse, the soldiers seize him and lead him toward his cross. They turn him around and push him down backward. His bloody and bruised body is slammed against the wood and the crown of thorns presses deeper into his head. There is no mercy in the hearts of these soldiers. To them Jesus is just another man deserving of death. They have a job to do, and a day's pay to look forward to when it is finished.

Jesus' arms and legs are extended. With a heavy hammer, a soldier pounds sharp wooden nails through his hands and feet. Blood spurts out and spills onto the ground. "A company of evil-doers encircle me; they have pierced my hands and feet—I can count all my bones—they stare and gloat over me" (Psalm 22:16-17). With great effort, the soldiers lift up the cross on which hangs the Savior of the world. It sways precariously to and fro as it is dropped into a hole. Jesus is positioned between the two criminals.

Raised high above the crowd, Jesus sees all those who are mocking him. Yet his heart is filled with mercy as he prays, "Father, forgive them; for they know not what they do" (Luke 23:34). As he says these words, he hears the harsh, taunting voice of one of the criminals. "Are you not the Christ? Save yourself and us!" The other criminal rebukes him: "Do you not fear God, since you are under the same sentence of condemnation? And we indeed justly; for we are receiving the due reward of our deeds; but this man has done nothing wrong." The condemned man is rewarded for his faith as Jesus tells him, "Truly, I say to you, today you will be with me in Paradise" (Luke 23:39-43).

Jesus, Who Are You?

You are the Suffering Servant. "The righteous one, my servant, shall make many righteous, and he shall bear their iniquities" (Isaiah 53:11). You predicted that you would suffer many things, be rejected by the elders, chief priests, and teachers of the law, and be killed (Mark 8:31). "Greater love has no man than this, that a man lay down his life for his friends" (John 15:13). Your prediction was fulfilled, and you, ever the servant, willingly laid down your life for me, a sinner. Thank you for all the suffering you endured on my behalf. I offer up my own suffering and join it to yours in your ongoing work of redemption.

Jesus, Show Me Your Face

You are merciful and forgiving. Jesus, you taught the crowds on the mountainside, "Blessed are the merciful, for they shall obtain mercy" (Matthew 5:7). You explained that we must forgive and be merciful seventy times seven (18:21-35). Jesus, the parable of the prodigal son is a mirror of the mercy and forgiveness that my heavenly Father offers to me when I return to him and repent of my sins (Luke 15:11-32). It is never too late to cry out to you for mercy. The thief hanging next to you received forgiveness and the promise of Paradise just as he was about to die (Luke 23:43). Jesus, look mercifully upon us all.

Jesus, I Repent

I come before you now to ask for your forgiveness and healing love. Jesus, from the cross you forgave those who were putting you to death. I repent for the times when I have not been merciful to others and have refused to forgive. Father, I bring to you all the people who have hurt me. To my mind, they are guilty and deserve punishment. But I want your heart, Father, and so I choose to freely give the gift of my forgiveness even to those I don't think deserve it. (Name each person individually.) Holy Spirit, heal me of all bitterness and resentment.

Jesus, I Pray

I turn to you in prayer and intercession. Jesus, *Suffering Servant*, I'm so grateful that you generously pour out mercy on all who repent of their sins. Thank you for all the times you have forgiven me.

At this **Eleventh Station** I pray for those who are close to death. Father, comfort them as they surrender themselves into your loving arms. Holy Spirit, for those who are dying and still need to repent, gently convict them of their sins so they can ask for and receive your infinite mercy.

Forgive us our trespasses, as we forgive those who trespass against us.
(The Lord's Prayer)

I adore you, O Christ,
and I praise you, because by your
holy cross you have redeemed
the world.

12

JESUS DIES ON THE CROSS

Jesus hangs suspended from the cross. Dark clouds cover the afternoon sun, making it seem like night. Obeying Pilate's orders, the soldiers have nailed a sign in Hebrew, Latin, and Greek on Jesus' cross. It reads, "Jesus of Nazareth, the King of the Jews" (John 19:19-22). Some in the crowd mock him, shouting, "If you are the Son of God, come down from the cross" (Matthew 27:40).

Mary is now standing at the foot of the cross of her beloved Son. She is not alone. John, the disciple who laid his head on Jesus' breast at the Last Supper, is also there. Jesus looks down at Mary and John. His words are few. "Woman, behold, your son!" "Behold, your mother!" (John 19:26-27). He entrusts them to each other's care. Jesus has given the Church her Mother.

Death from crucifixion is agonizingly slow. Its victims eventually die of asphyxia. Three excruciating hours pass. Alone and abandoned, Jesus suffers emotionally and mentally as well as physically. Quoting from his beloved psalms, he cries out, "My God, my God, why have you forsaken me?" (Matthew 27:46; Psalm 22:1). His dry, parched throat is on fire. "I thirst" (John 19:28). A Roman soldier soaks a sponge in vinegar, places it on a reed of hyssop, and holds it up to his mouth. "For my thirst they gave me vinegar to drink" (Psalm 69:21).

The time has come. "It is finished" (John 19:30). Jesus surrenders his life into his loving Father's hands (Luke 23:46). He bows his head and dies for the salvation of the world. The curtain of the temple is torn in two from top to bottom. The earth shakes and the rocks split (Matthew 27:51). "God proves his love for us in that while we still were sinners Christ died for us" (Romans 5:8). (Take a few minutes to thank Jesus for dying for you.)

Jesus, Who Are You?

You are Savior of the World. Everyone has sinned and is in need of a Savior. Jesus, I am a sinner, yet you desire a personal relationship with me. You stand at the door of my heart and knock (Revelation 3:20). Jesus, I invite you to come into my life. Jesus, I know that I can have victory over the sins in my life if I cling to your cross. Through the waters of baptism, I can say, "I have been crucified with Christ; it is no longer I who live, but Christ who lives in me" (Galatians 2:20). Jesus, when you died on the cross, the reign of Satan came to an end. I proclaim the victory of your cross in my life and in those I love (Romans 6, 7, and 8).

Jesus, Show Me Your Face

You are loving. Jesus, you are the perfect revelation of divine love. "In this the love of God was made manifest among us, that God sent his only Son into the world, so that we might live through him" (1 John 4:9). The cross is the sign of your perfect love. You love as a bridegroom loves his bride (John 3:29), personally and unconditionally. Jesus, so many people do not know your love. Please give me an opportunity today to tell someone how much you love and care for them.

Jesus, I Repent

I come before you now to ask for your forgiveness and healing love. Jesus, for the times in my life that I sought fulfillment from things other than you—money, possessions, sexual relationships, or prestige—forgive me. I repent of my sins of arrogance and independence in choosing to live my life as I wanted. Holy Spirit, I ask you to heal me of any doubts or insecurities that would lead me to believe I cannot be part of God's family. Father, I know you have a plan for my life (Jeremiah 29:11).

Jesus, I Pray

I turn to you in prayer and intercession. Jesus, *Savior*, you died so that we may have eternal life. Help me to share the good news of your saving love with everyone I know.

At this **Twelfth Station** I pray for all those who have not repented of their sins and experienced conversion. Holy Spirit, soften the hearts of those who are cynical or hardened about your love for them, especially prisoners. Bring into the fullness of truth all those who do not know or cannot accept Jesus as Son of God and Savior of the world.

Through him, with him, in him, in the unity of the Holy Spirit, all glory and honor is yours, almighty Father, forever and ever.

(Doxology of the Eucharistic Prayer)

I adore you, O Christ,
and I praise you, because by your
holy cross you have redeemed
the world.

Mary gazes up at the lifeless body of her beloved Son. The apostle John, who has been entrusted with Mary's care, is at her side. The shouts and jeering of the crowd have given way to an eerie silence. The soldiers are anxious to finish their work, so they break the legs of the two thieves in order to hasten their deaths. Jesus is already dead, so they decide not to break his bones. "Not one of them [his bones] is broken" (Psalm 34:20). Instead, a soldier takes his sword and pierces Jesus' side. Out gushes blood and water (John 19:31-37).

It is the eve of the sabbath. Jesus' body must be removed quickly, as the law requires that it be buried before the sun sets. What will happen to Jesus? God has provided for his dead Son. He has given courage to Joseph of Arimathea, a Pharisee and a secret follower of Jesus, to ask permission from Pilate for the body of Jesus (Luke 23:50-52). This is granted. A ladder is placed up against the cross of Jesus. The nails are gently removed from his hands and feet. With sheets Jesus is slowly lowered to the ground.

Mary prepares to receive her son. She opens her arms as she opened her heart when the Holy Spirit overshadowed her (Luke 1:35). Jesus' body is placed in her arms. Lovingly she cradles the tortured and lifeless body of her beloved Son. She remembers the day so many years ago when she cradled the warm, soft body of her infant. Grief overtakes her. Mary, Queen of Sorrows, pray for us.

Jesus, Who Are You?

You are the Great High Priest. In Israel, the high priest offered an atoning sacrifice for the sins of his people. Jesus, you are the perfect High Priest, whose sacrifice once and for all atoned for humanity's sins. You are a priest forever (Hebrews 7:21), who continues to intercede for us. "He is able for all time to save those who approach God through him, since he always lives to make intercession for them" (7:25). Intercession was such an important part of your relationship with your Father (Luke 22:31-32; John 17). Even on the cross you asked your Father to forgive your executioners (Luke 23:34). Jesus, I ask for an intercessor's heart.

Jesus, Show Me Your Face

You are omnipresent. Jesus, through your death you conquered death forever. You are "the resurrection and the life" (John 11:25). You are present in the Blessed Sacrament in every tabernacle of the world. In every heart that proclaims you as Lord, you make your home. Jesus, you are the Alpha and the Omega, who is, who was, and who is to come (Revelation 1:8). Even if we try, we can't hide from your presence (Psalm 139:7). You are everywhere!

Jesus, I Repent

I come before you now to ask for your forgiveness and healing. Jesus, forgive me for the times when I believed the lies of Satan—that you don't love me, that I'm worthless, or that you died for everyone but me. Holy Spirit, heal me of any painful memories of rejection, abandonment, or abuse. I ask you, Jesus, to be with me in those memories. I imagine you standing beside me, smiling at me and telling me, "It's okay. I'm here." Jesus, I receive healing as I sit in your presence. Father, I trust, hope, and absorb your incredible love for me!

Jesus, I Pray

Jesus, I turn to you in prayer and intercession. Jesus, *Great High Priest*, I am full of gratitude for your atoning sacrifice. Thank you for interceding for me today before the throne of God. Help me to become a faithful intercessor.

At this *Thirteenth Station* I pray for all evangelists who tell others about Jesus Christ and the power of his life, death, and resurrection. Holy Spirit, protect missionaries who risk their lives by preaching in countries where Christians are persecuted and often martyred.

Dying, you destroyed our death.
Rising, you restored our life.
Lord Jesus, come in glory.
(Memorial Acclamation after the Consecration)

I adore you, O Christ,
and I praise you, because by your
holy cross you have redeemed
the world.

As Mary holds Jesus, she is approached by Joseph of Arimathea and Nicodemus, the Pharisee who had come to Jesus at night (John 3:1-21; 7:50-52). Time is short, they explain, and the burial must soon take place. Gently Jesus is lifted out of Mary's arms. A final sword pierces her heart as she is separated from her beloved Son. They place Jesus' body on sheets and carry him to a nearby garden, where there is a tomb belonging to Joseph of Arimathea that has been newly cut out of the rock. Mary, John, and some of the women comfort one another as they accompany Jesus' body to its resting place.

Nicodemus has brought a mixture of myrrh and aloes to anoint the body (John 19:39-40). They must be quick, as it is almost sundown. There is time only to wrap Jesus' body in strips of linen cloth, together with the spices. Jesus is then laid in the tomb. A large stone is rolled against the opening (Mark 15:46). Mary Magdalene and some of the other women plan to return to solemnly anoint Jesus' body with more spices after the Passover, on the first day of the week (Matthew 27:59-61).

Jesus, Who Are You?

You are the Light of the World. You said, "I am the light of the world; he who follows me will not walk in darkness, but will have the light of life" (John 8:12). Jesus, you came to bring us out of darkness into your marvelous light (1 Peter 2:9). By your death on the cross, Satan, the prince of darkness, has been defeated. Holy Spirit, I choose to fight the spiritual battle with the sword of the Spirit, the word of God (Ephesians 6:17). Help me to recall the truths of Scripture in times of temptation. Jesus, my goal is to walk as a child of the light in a world that is sometimes very dark.

Jesus, Show Me Your Face

You are immutable and unchanging. Jesus, you are the same "yesterday and today and for ever" (Hebrews 13:8). Everything around me may change, but you remain the same (Psalm 102:26-27). Jesus, I make myself present to your presence. I bow down before you. I proclaim you King of kings and Lord of lords. I join with everyone in heaven before your throne proclaiming: "Worthy is the Lamb who was slain, to receive power and wealth and wisdom and might and honor and glory and blessing!" (Revelation 5:12).

Jesus, I Repent

I come before you now to ask for your forgiveness and healing love. Jesus, I ask forgiveness for forgetting that my heavenly Father's love is unchanging. Father, even when I feel depressed, lonely, or worthless, the truth is that my name is written on the palms of your hands (Isaiah 49:16). I have been deeply loved from the moment of my conception. Holy Spirit, heal me as I imagine my heavenly Father wrapping his arms around me and saying, "I love you, _____" (insert your own name).

Jesus, I Pray

I turn to you in prayer and intercession. Jesus, *Light of the World*, you are the light that shines in the darkness (John 1:5). Help me to carry your light into every situation in which you place me.

At this *Fourteenth Station* I pray for all those who have died, especially those in purgatory who have no one to pray for them. Eternal rest give unto them, O Lord, and let perpetual light shine upon them. May the souls of the faithful departed, through the mercy of God, rest in peace. Amen.

Lord, by your cross and resurrection,
you have set us free. You are the
Savior of the world.

(Memorial Acclamation after the Consecration)

A Litany in Praise of Jesus' Resurrection

Early on the first day of the week, while it was still dark, Mary Magdalene came to the garden and saw that the stone had been removed from the tomb. (John 20:1)

Alleluia! With a joyful heart, I recall your wondrous power, O Lord!

So she ran and went to Simon Peter and the other disciple, the one whom Jesus loved, and said to them, "They have taken the Lord out of the tomb, and we do not know where they have laid him." (John 20:2)

Alleluia! With a joyful heart, I recall your wondrous power, O Lord!

Then Peter and the other disciple set out and went toward the tomb. . . . He saw the linen wrappings lying there, and the cloth that had been on Jesus' head, not lying with the linen wrappings but rolled up in a place by itself. Then the other disciple, who reached the tomb first, also went in, and he saw and believed. (John 20:3, 6-8)

Alleluia! With a joyful heart, I recall your wondrous power, O Lord!

But Mary stood weeping outside the tomb. As she wept, she bent over to look into the tomb; and she saw two angels. . . . They said to her, "Woman, why are you weeping?" She said to them, "They have taken away my Lord, and I do not know where they have laid him." (John 20:11-13)

Alleluia! With a joyful heart, I recall your wondrous power, O Lord!

When she had said this, she turned around and saw Jesus standing there. . . . Jesus said to her, "Mary!" She turned and said to him in Hebrew, Rabbouni!" (John 20:14, 16)

Alleluia! With a joyful heart, I recall your wondrous power, O Lord!

Jesus said to her, "Do not hold on to me, because I have not yet ascended to the Father. But go to my brothers and say to them, 'I am ascending to my

Father and your Father, to my God and your God.'"
Mary Magdalene went and announced to the disciples, "I have seen the Lord." (John 20:17-18)

Alleluia! With a joyful heart, I recall your wondrous power, O Lord!

After his suffering he presented himself alive to them by many convincing proofs, appearing to them during forty days and speaking about the kingdom of God. (Acts 1:3)

Alleluia! With a joyful heart, I recall your wondrous power, O Lord!

"You will receive power when the Holy Spirit has come upon you; and you will be my witnesses in Jerusalem, in all Judea and Samaria, and to the ends of the earth." (Acts 1:8)

Alleluia! With a joyful heart, I recall your wondrous power, O Lord!

When he had said this, as they were watching, he was lifted up, and a cloud took him out of their sight. (Acts 1:9)

Alleluia! With a joyful heart, I recall your wondrous power, O Lord!

When the day of Pentecost had come, they were all together in one place. And suddenly from heaven there came a sound like the rush of a violent wind. . . . All of them were filled with the Holy Spirit and began to speak in other languages, as the Spirit gave them ability. (Acts 2:1-2, 4)

Alleluia! With a joyful heart, I recall your wondrous power, O Lord!

About the Artwork

Giandomenico Tiepolo (1727-1804) painted these Stations of the Cross for the Oratory of the Crucified Christ at the Church of San Polo in Venice, where they can still be seen today. He was only twenty years old when he received this commission. Tiepolo was trained as an artist in the studio of his famous father, Giovanni Battista Tiepolo, who was considered the greatest Italian painter of the eighteenth century. In their Venetian workshop, father and son often collaborated on works, making accurate attribution difficult at times. Gradually, however, Giandomenico developed his own personal style. He is famous for the frescos he painted for the guest lodge at Villa Valmarana near Vicenza. He is also noted for his etchings, especially those depicting the Flight into Egypt, which were completed in 1753.

ABOUT THE AUTHOR

Angela M. Burrin is the director of Partners in Evangelism, a ministry of The Word Among Us, Inc. Partners sends out free copies of *The Word Among Us* magazine to more than 30,000 Catholic prisoners and 10,000 service men and women in the military each month. Angela has authored spiritual materials specifically for prisoners, including *God Alone: Stories of the Power of Faith,* and *God Forgives . . . Can I?* This book, *Step by Step to Calvary,* was also written originally for prisoners.

Prior to joining Partners, Angela spent nineteen years in the field of education as a teacher—ten years in Kent, England, and nine years as the founding principal of the Mother of God School in Maryland. She is a volunteer at the Maryland Correctional Institute for Women and at Gift of Peace, the residential home run by the Missionaries of Charity in Washington, D.C.

Also From The Word Among Us Press

The Mysteries of Christ: A Scriptural Rosary
Includes the new Mysteries of Light and reflections
by Pope John Paul II
Compiled by Nancy Sabbag

The rosary is a treasured tradition of the church, "a marvelous prayer" in the words of Pope John Paul II. In his Letter on the Rosary, the Holy Father urged a revival of this time-honored method of Christian contemplation and introduced a new set of mysteries, the Mysteries of Light. He also suggested "the proclamation of related biblical passages" as an accompaniment to each mystery as a way of allowing God to speak to us as we pray. *The Mysteries of Christ: A Scriptural Rosary* features pertinent Scripture verses from both the Old and New Testament for each *Our Father* and *Hail Mary* for all twenty mysteries of the rosary. Also included:

- Colorful artwork by Flemish Renaissance painter Simon Bening illustrating *each* of the twenty mysteries
- Excerpts of Pope John Paul II's Letter on the Rosary
- An article explaining how the rosary engages both our minds and bodies in prayer

Item # BROSE3